ACCENT ON ACHIEVEMENT

John
O'Reilly
and
Mark
Williams

A comprehensive band method that develops creativity and musicianship

Dear Band Student:

Congratulations on completing the first book of **ACCENT ON ACHIEVEMENT**. You have already learned a great deal and are well on your way to becoming an accomplished musician. Book 2 will take you even further on this journey. You will play more great music by composers you've already studied, plus 14 new composers. In addition, you'll play rock, jazz, Latin and ragtime pieces, along with fantastic folk songs from around the world. Practice diligently, and you are sure to do great things in the fascinating world of music.

John O'Reilly　　*Mark Williams*

John O'Reilly　　　　Mark Williams

Illustrations: Martin Ledyard

Instrument photos (cover and p.1) are courtesy of Yamaha Corporation of America.

ACCENT ON REVIEW

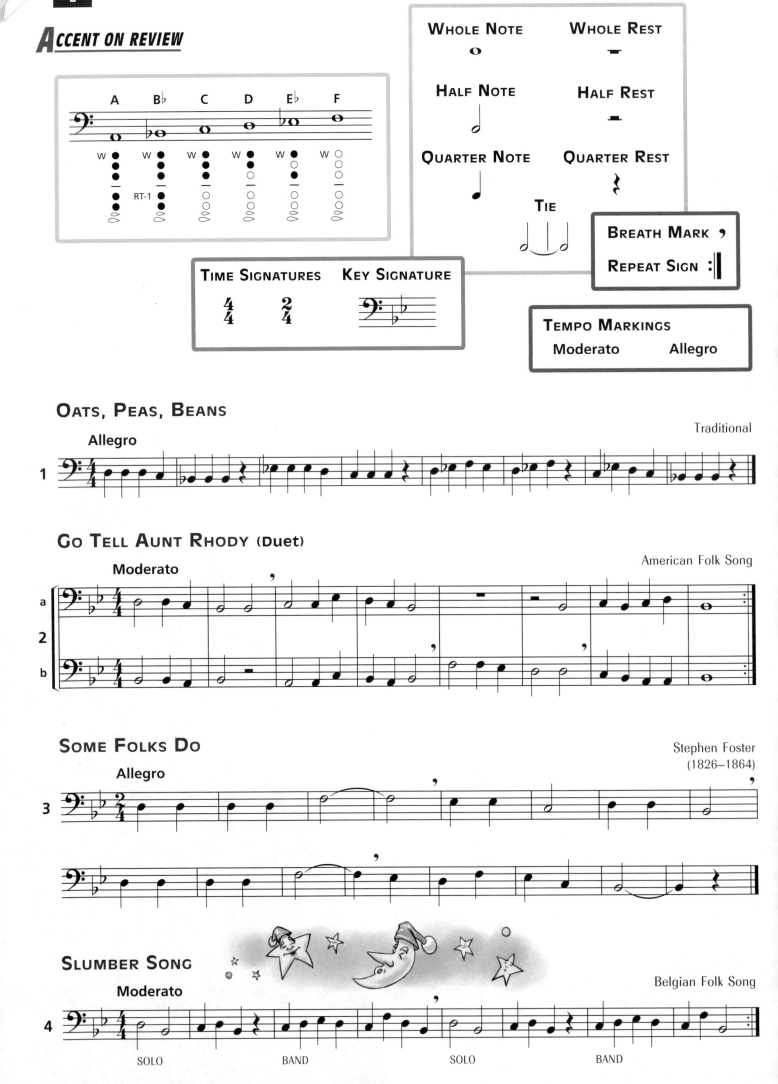

Accent on Review

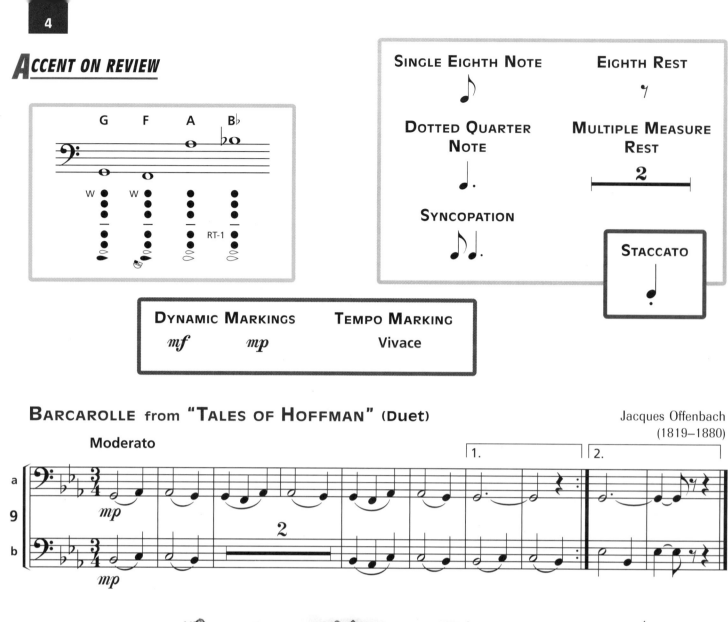

Barcarolle from "Tales of Hoffman" (Duet)

Jacques Offenbach
(1819–1880)

Deck the Halls

Traditional Carol

Billy Boy

American Folk Song

ACCENT ON REVIEW

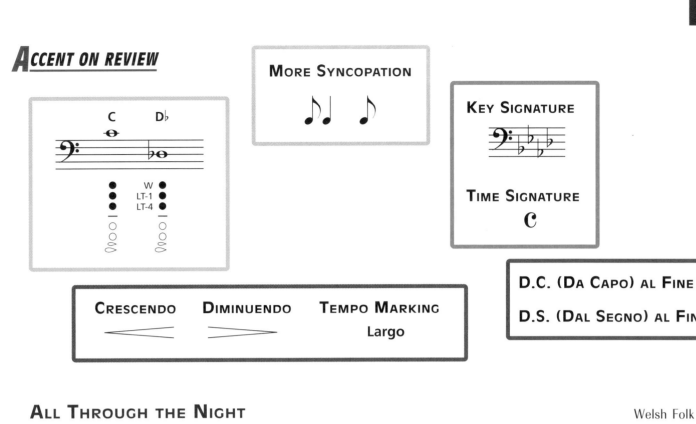

ACCENT ON PERFORMANCE

MARCH ONWARD

John O'Reilly and Mark Williams

TIME SIGNATURE ¢

Cut Time—same as $\frac{2}{2}$

$\frac{2}{2}$ = 2 beats in each measure
$\frac{2}{2}$ = half note receives 1 beat

TEMPO MARKING
Allegretto
Moderately fast tempo

HALF NOTE GETS THE BEAT

Moderato

16

mf

Count: 1 & 2 & 1 & 2 &

SING NOEL (ROUND)

Allegretto

Liberian Folk Song

17

f

SCARBOROUGH FAIR

English Folk Song

Andante

18

p < mp < mf

> mp > p

HIGH SCHOOL CADETS

John Philip Sousa
(1854–1932)

Allegro

19

f 2 &

1 &

ACCENT ON BASSOON

20

mf

For more individual technique practice, see page 42, #1.

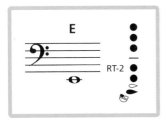

HALF STEP/WHOLE STEP

On a piano keyboard, the distance between any two adjacent keys is called a half step. Two half steps equal one whole step.

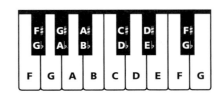

A to B♭ = 1/2 step
A to B = whole step
B to C = 1/2 step
B♭ to C = whole step

DIFFERENT STEPS

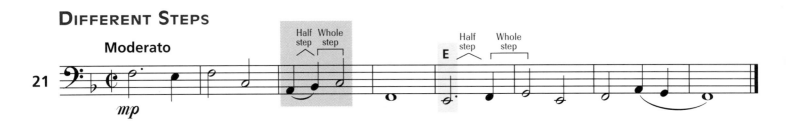

UP ON THE HOUSETOP

Traditional Carol

ZUM GALI GALI (Duet)

Israeli Folk Song

ACCENT ON THEORY: Identifying Half Steps and Whole Steps

Label all half steps with ⌃. Label all whole steps with ⌐⌐.

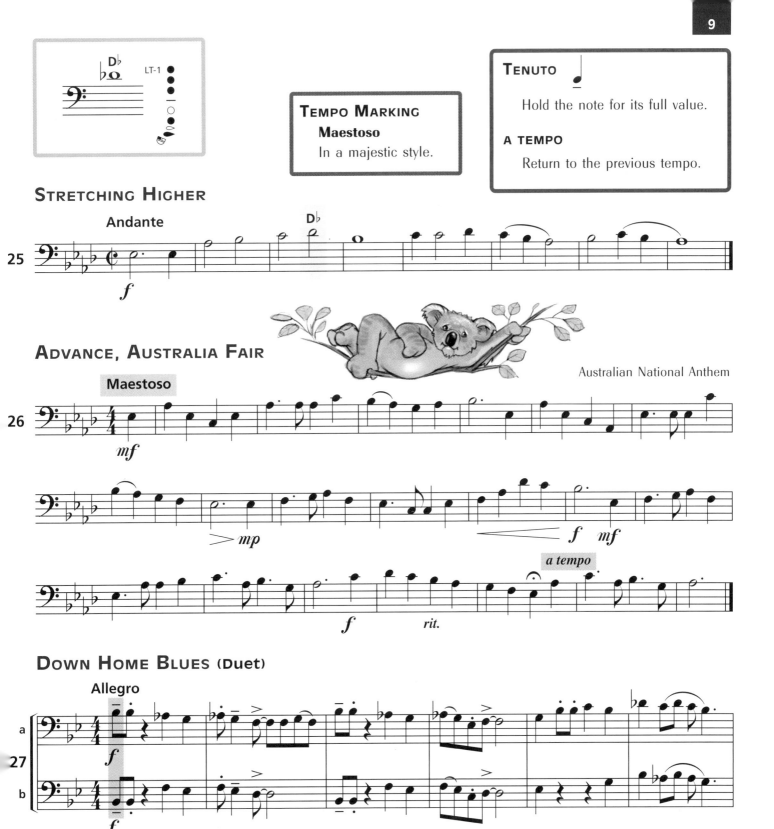

STRETCHING HIGHER

Andante

25

ADVANCE, AUSTRALIA FAIR

Maestoso

Australian National Anthem

26

mf

mp

f *mf*

a tempo

f *rit.*

DOWN HOME BLUES (Duet)

Allegro

27

f

f

div.

ACCENT ON CREATIVITY: *Free Rhythmic Improvisation*

28   Improvise about eight measures of rhythms using any combination of hand claps, finger snaps
and foot stomps. Try to maintain a steady tempo while varying the rhythms and sounds.

SIXTEENTH NOTES

Receive 1/4 beat in 2/4, 3/4 and 4/4 time.

1 e & a 2 e & a

FOUR TO THE BEAT

Moderato

29

mf

Count: 1 e & a 2 & 3 &

THE THUNDERER

John Philip Sousa
(1854–1932)

Allegro

30

f

HARVEST SONG

Estonian Folk Song

Allegretto

31

mp   *mf*   *mp*

mf   *f*   *>*

SIMPLE GIFTS

American Folk Song

Moderato

32

mf

Fine

D.S. al Fine

f   *mf*

ACCENT ON BASSOON

33

mp

For more individual technique practice, see page 42, #2.

ACCENT ON PERFORMANCE

HOLIDAY FANTASY

Arranged by
John O'Reilly and Mark Williams

AFTER-BEATS

$\frac{2}{4}$ ♪ ♪ ♪ ♪
1 & 2 &

KEY SIGNATURE

There are no sharps or flats in the key of C.

TRANSPOSING

Rewriting a melody beginning on a different starting pitch, maintaining the same pattern of half steps and whole steps.

MINOR EPISODE

Moderato

34

AMERICA/GOD SAVE THE QUEEN

Andante

Traditional

35

THE OLD BRASS WAGON (Duet)

Allegro

American Folk Song

36

a

b

THEME FROM "A MIDSUMMER NIGHT'S DREAM"

Felix Mendelssohn
(1809–1847)

Allegretto

37

Count: 1 e & a 2 &

ACCENT ON THEORY

Transpose the first 6 measures of #35 (America/God Save the Queen) into these two keys, then play.

38

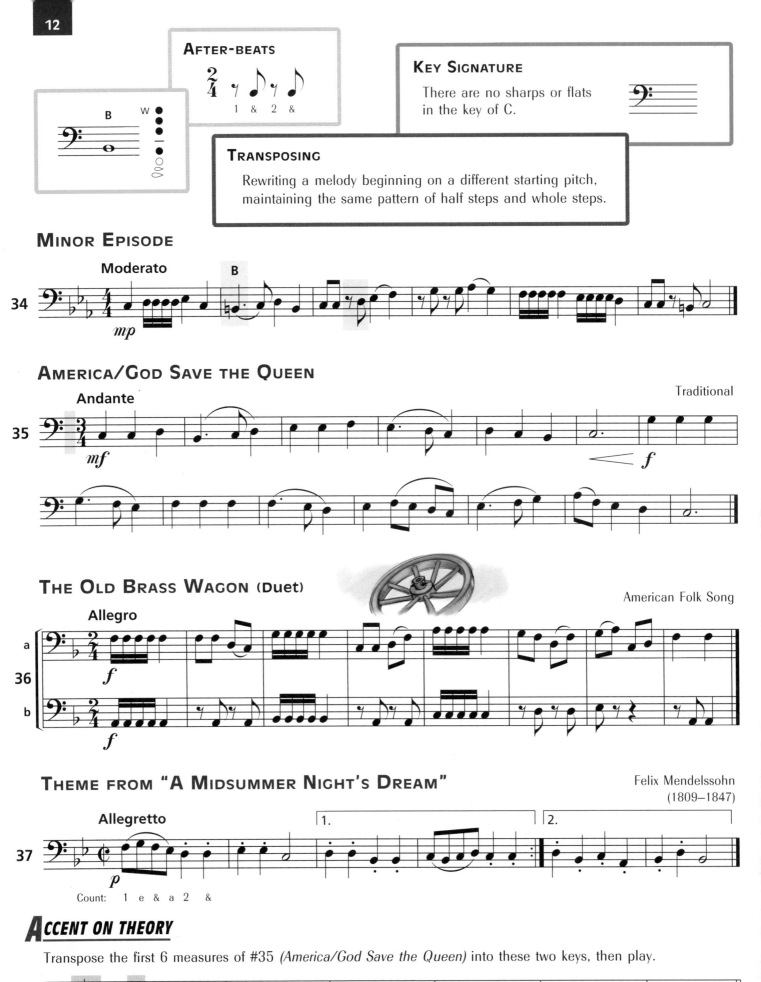

AN EIGHTH NOTE AND TWO SIXTEENTHS

1 (e) & a   2 (e) & a

DYNAMIC MARKING
f–p

Play *f* the first time, and *p* the second time.

HIGH NOTE HAPPENING
Moderato

SIXTEENTH AVENUE
Allegretto

EL FLORON (Duet)
Mexican Folk Song
Allegro

THE PAWPAW PATCH
American Folk Song
Moderato

SPRING from "THE FOUR SEASONS"
Antonio Vivaldi (1678–1741)
Allegretto

ACCENT ON CREATIVITY: *Passing Tones and Neighbor Tones*

Write your own variation on this theme by adding passing tones (notes between pitches a third apart) and neighbor tones (above or below repeated pitches).

P.T.   N.T.

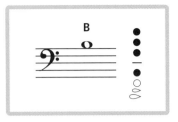

MORE SIXTEENTHS

45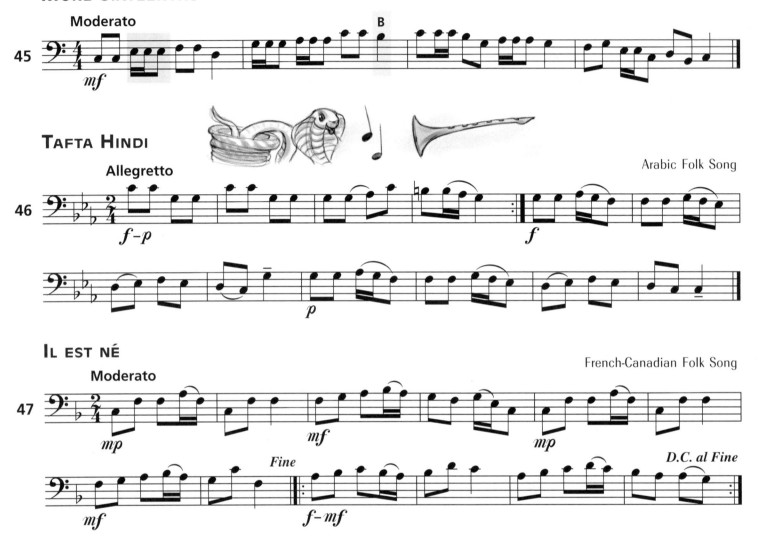

TAFTA HINDI

Arabic Folk Song

IL EST NÉ

French-Canadian Folk Song

PAT-A-PAN

French Folk Song

For more individual technique practice, see page 42, #3 & 4.

> **DOTTED EIGHTH NOTE**
>
> Receives 3/4 beat in **2/4**, **3/4** and **4/4** time.

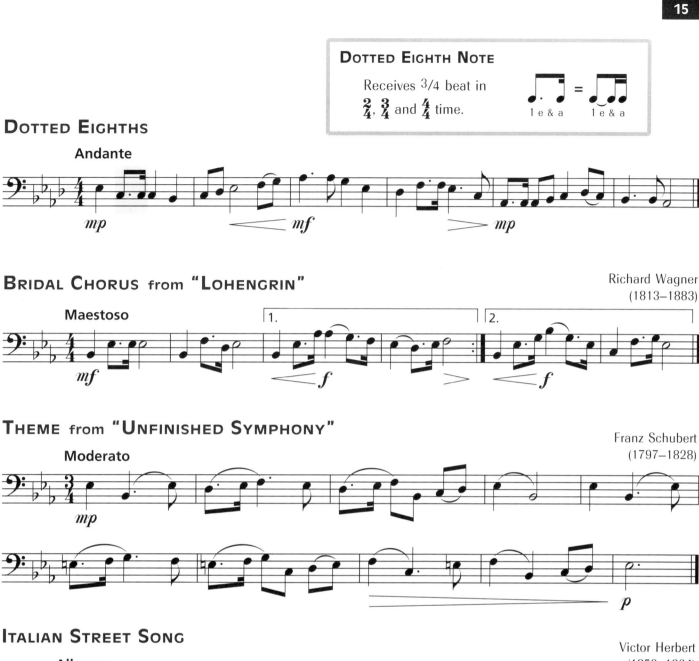

DOTTED EIGHTHS

Andante

50

mp   < *mf*   > *mp*

BRIDAL CHORUS from "LOHENGRIN"

Richard Wagner
(1813–1883)

Maestoso

51

mf   < *f*   >   < *f*

THEME from "UNFINISHED SYMPHONY"

Franz Schubert
(1797–1828)

Moderato

52

mp

p

ITALIAN STREET SONG

Victor Herbert
(1859–1924)

Allegro

53

f

> *mp*

f

ACCENT ON THEORY   MAJOR SCALE CONSTRUCTION: All major scales contain the same pattern of whole steps and half steps. Study this pattern in the example below. Now build your own major scale beginning on the note given, adding any sharps or flats as necessary. Note names must be in alphabetical order.

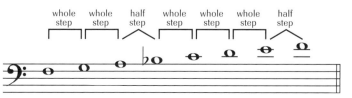

whole step — whole step — half step — whole step — whole step — whole step — half step

54

Accent on Performance

Cyberspace Overture

John O'Reilly and Mark Williams

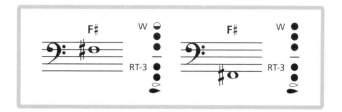

LOOKING SHARP

Largo

55

O CANADA

Canadian National Anthem

Maestoso

56

ARIA from "THE MARRIAGE OF FIGARO"

Wolfgang A. Mozart
(1756–1791)

Allegretto

57

ACCENT ON CREATIVITY: *Improvisation on Chord Changes*

Improvise your own melody using the notes contained in each triad (three-note chord).
You may also use passing or neighbor tones as long as they are of short duration.

58

D.C. (DA CAPO) AL CODA

Go back to the beginning;
then skip to the coda.

RANGE BUILDER

Moderato

59 *mf*

FLOWER DRUM SONG

Chinese Folk Song

Andante

60 *mp*

mf *mp*

**Flicking: See explanation on page 42, #3.

NU ÄR DET JUL IGEN

Swedish Folk Song

Moderato

61 *mf*

COLONEL BOGEY

Kenneth Alford
(1881–1945)

Allegro *To Coda* ⊕

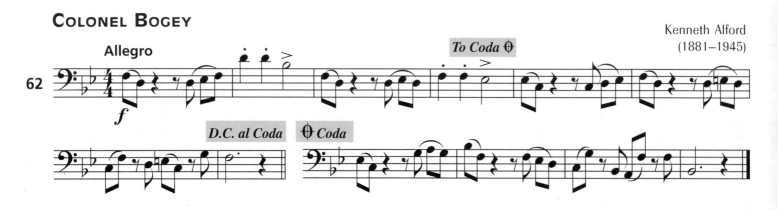

62 *f*

D.C. al Coda ⊕ *Coda*

Accent on Bassoon

63 *mf*

For more individual technique practice, see page 42, #5 and page 43, #6.

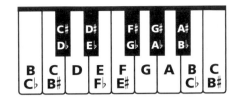

ENHARMONICS

Any two notes that are written differently, but sound the same.

C# = Db
F# = Gb
B = Cb

CHROMATIC CRAWL

64

THEME from "PIANO CONCERTO NO. 2"

Sergei Rachmaninoff
(1873–1943)

65

Andante

mp

**Flicking: See page 42, #3.

IN THE HALL OF THE MOUNTAIN KING

Edvard Grieg
(1843–1907)

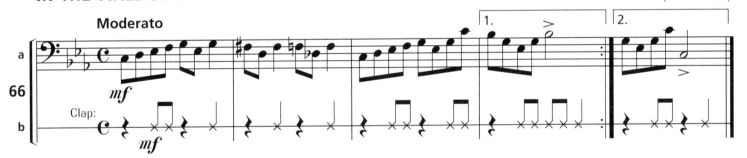

66

OVERTURE from "THE BARBER OF SEVILLE"

Gioacchino Rossini
(1792–1868)

67

ACCENT ON THEORY   Rewrite each of these notes as its enharmonic equivalent.

68

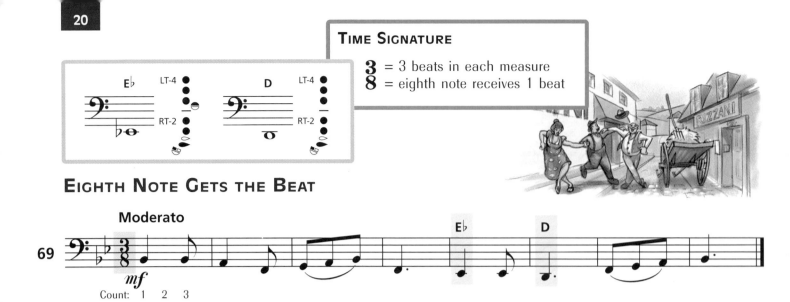

TIME SIGNATURE

$\frac{3}{8}$ = 3 beats in each measure
= eighth note receives 1 beat

EIGHTH NOTE GETS THE BEAT

Moderato

69

mf

Count: 1 2 3

TARANTELLA (Duet)

Italian Folk Song

Allegro

a
70
b

f

f

a
mp
b
mp

BATTLE HYMN OF THE REPUBLIC

Traditional

Maestoso

70

mf

f

ACCENT ON CREATIVITY: *Composition Based on a Rhythmic Pattern*

Write your own short composition, using the rhythmic pattern ♪♩ in different ways.
Be sure to include: 1) clef sign 2) key signature 3) time signature. Play your composition.

72

ACCENT ON PERFORMANCE

WATER MUSIC

George F. Handel (1685–1759)
Arr. by John O'Reilly and Mark Williams

TIME SIGNATURE

6 = 6 beats in each measure
8 = eighth note receives 1 beat

D.S. (DAL SEGNO) AL CODA

Go back to the sign 𝄋;
then skip to the coda.

SIX TO THE BAR

Andante

73

mp

Count: 1 2 3 4 5 6   1 2 3 4 5 6

ROW, ROW, ROW YOUR BOAT (Round)

American Folk Song

Moderato   ①   ②   ③

74

mf

I'S THE B'Y (Duet)

Canadian Folk Song
(Newfoundland)

Allegretto

a

75

f

b

f

THE ENTERTAINER

Scott Joplin
(1868–1917)

Allegro 𝄋   *To Coda* ⊕

76

mf   *f*   *mf*

D.S. al Coda

f

mf

⊕ *Coda*

mf   *f*

ACCENT ON BASSOON

77

mf

For more individual technique practice, see page 43, #7.

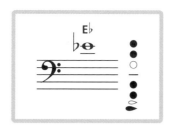

TEMPO MARKING

Andantino

Slightly faster than Andante.

STILL HIGHER

CALYPSO CLIMB (Duet)

I SAW THREE SHIPS

Traditional Carol

THE STAR-SPANGLED BANNER

U.S. National Anthem

ACCENT ON THEORY   Rewrite the following example in cut time.

MOLTO RIT.

Dramatically slow down the tempo.

SMOOTH SLURRING

Andantino

83

mp *mf* *p*

**Flicking: See page 42, #3.

HABAÑERA from "CARMEN"

Moderato

Georges Bizet
(1838–1875)

84

mp

p

YODELING SONG

Austrian Folk Song

Allegretto

85

a

f

Clap:

b

f

1.   2.

THEME from "VIOLIN CONCERTO IN D"

Ludwig van Beethoven
(1770–1827)

Allegretto

86

mf

D.C. al Fine

Fine

mp

p *molto rit.*

ACCENT ON CREATIVITY: *Improvisation on a Blues Scale*

Using the pitches shown, improvise your own melody using any rhythms you know.
You may play these notes in any order, repeat notes, or use rests.

87

TEMPO MARKING
Adagio
Slightly slower than Andante.

SFORZANDO *sfz*
A strong accent.

CLOG DANCE

HOPAK from "THE FAIR AT SOROCHINSK"

Modest Mussorgsky
(1839–1881)

O TANNENBAUM

German Folk Song

BLOW AWAY THE MORNING DEW

English Folk Song

ACCENT ON BASSOON

For more individual technique practice, see page 43, #8.

ACCENT ON PERFORMANCE

FIESTA **M**EXICALI

John O'Reilly and Mark Williams

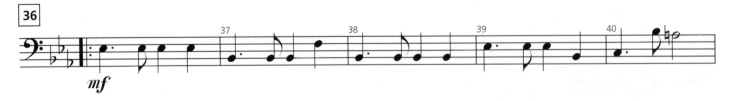

DYNAMIC MARKINGS

pp   *ff*

Pianissimo—very soft   Fortissimo—very loud

BEAMING OVER A REST

BEAM ME UP

Allegretto

93

THE SORCERER'S APPRENTICE

Paul Dukas
(1865–1935)

Vivace

94

COUNTRY GARDENS (Duet)

English Folk Song

Moderato

a

95

b

a

b

ACCENT ON THEORY

Draw the correct bar lines, then write in the counting and clap.

96

KEY SIGNATURE

All B's, E's, A's, D's and G's should be played as Bb, Eb, Ab, Db and Gb throughout.

MULTIPLE FLATS

Adagio

97

mp

OVER THE RIVER AND THROUGH THE WOODS

American Folk Song

Allegretto

98

mf

MARCH OF THE TOREADORS

Georges Bizet
(1838–1875)

Moderato

99

f

mf

f

FUM, FUM, FUM

Traditional Spanish Carol

Allegro

100

f

mf

f

ACCENT ON CREATIVITY: *Extended Composition*

101 Write your own composition of any length, using a separate sheet of music paper. Use some repeated rhythmic and/or melodic patterns to create unity. Use some contrasting material to create variety. Play your composition.

EIGHTH NOTE TRIPLETS

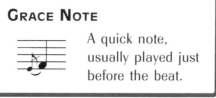

GRACE NOTE

A quick note, usually played just before the beat.

THREE TO THE BEAT

Moderato

102

mf

TRIPLET SONG

Andantino

French Folk Song

103

mp

p

mf

FINALE from "NEW WORLD SYMPHONY"

Allegro

Antonin Dvořák
(1841–1904)

104

ff

Fine

D.C. al Fine

mf

PROCESSION OF THE NOBLES

Maestoso

Nicolai Rimsky-Korsakov
(1844–1908)

105

f

ff

ACCENT ON BASSOON

106

mf

For more individual technique practice, see page 43, #9.

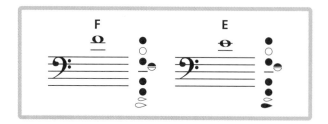

THE OUTER LIMITS

NOW IS THE MONTH OF MAYING (Duet)

Thomas Morley
(1559–1602)

LA DONNA É MOBILE

Giuseppe Verdi
(1813–1901)

SOLDIER'S CHORUS from "FAUST"

Charles Gounod
(1818–1893)

MARCH from "NUTCRACKER"

Peter Ilyich Tchaikovsky
(1840–1893)

For more individual technique practice, see page 43, #10.

ACCENT ON PERFORMANCE

SOUSA ON PARADE

John Philip Sousa
(1854–1932)
Arr. by John O'Reilly
and Mark Williams

*B*ASSOON SOLO

THE RAKES OF MALLOW

Arr. by John O'Reilly and Mark Williams

ACCENT ON ENSEMBLES

JAZZ FOR A SATURDAY AFTERNOON

John O'Reilly and Mark Williams

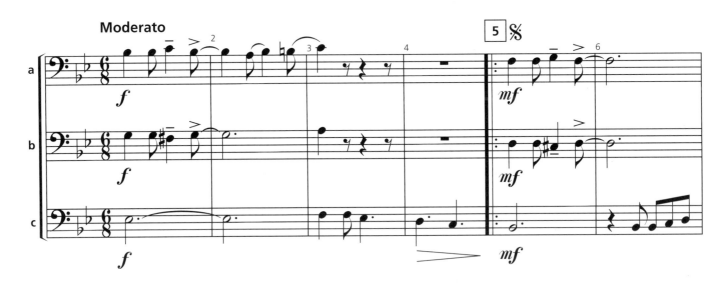

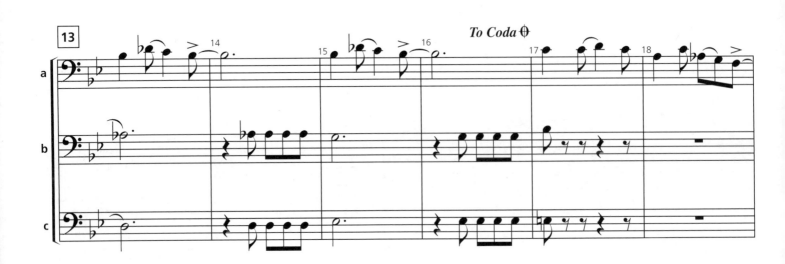

ACCENT ON SCALES

B♭ MAJOR SCALE (Concert B♭)

G HARMONIC MINOR SCALE (Concert G)

G MELODIC MINOR SCALE (Concert G)

F MAJOR SCALE (Concert F)

D HARMONIC MINOR SCALE (Concert D)

D MELODIC MINOR SCALE (Concert D)

E♭ MAJOR SCALE (Concert E♭)

C HARMONIC MINOR SCALE (Concert C)

C MELODIC MINOR SCALE (Concert C)

A♭ Major Scale (Concert A♭)

F Harmonic Minor Scale (Concert F)

F Melodic Minor Scale (Concert F)

C Major Scale (Concert C)

A Harmonic Minor Scale (Concert A)

A Melodic Minor Scale (Concert A)

D♭ Major Scale (Concert D♭)

B♭ Harmonic Minor Scale (Concert B♭)

B♭ Melodic Minor Scale (Concert B♭)

Chromatic Scale (Bassoons only)

ACCENT ON RHYTHMS

ACCENT ON RESTS

ACCENT ON BASSOON

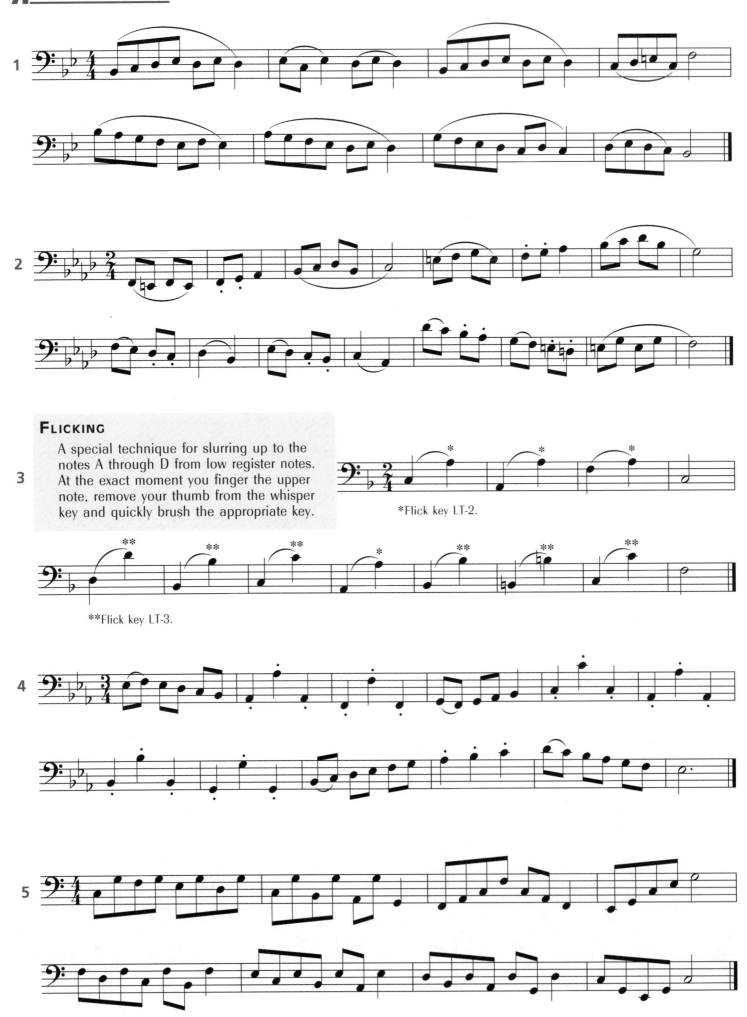

FLICKING

A special technique for slurring up to the notes A through D from low register notes. At the exact moment you finger the upper note, remove your thumb from the whisper key and quickly brush the appropriate key.

*Flick key LT-2.

**Flick key LT-3.

*Flick key LT-2.
**Flick key LT-3.

ACCENT ON CHORALES

WE GATHER TOGETHER

Netherlands Folk Song

NOW THANK WE ALL OUR GOD

Johann Sebastian Bach
(1685–1750)

MA-OZ TSUR (ROCK OF AGES)

Traditional Hanukkah Song

ALL THROUGH THE NIGHT

Welsh Folk Song

ETERNAL FATHER, STRONG TO SAVE

Navy Hymn

GLOSSARY

ACCENT (>) Play the note stronger

ADAGIO Slightly slower than Andante

ALFORD, KENNETH English composer (1881–1945)

ALLEGRETTO Moderately fast tempo

ALLEGRO Fast tempo

ANDANTE Moderately slow tempo

ANDANTINO Slightly faster than Andante

A TEMPO Return to the previous tempo

BACH, JOHANN SEBASTIAN German composer (1685–1750)

BEETHOVEN, LUDWIG VAN German composer (1770–1827)

BIZET, GEORGES French composer (1838–1875)

COMMON TIME (**C**) Same as $\frac{4}{4}$ time signature

CUT TIME (**¢**) Same as $\frac{2}{2}$ time signature

CRESCENDO (⊂) Get louder gradually

D.C. (DA CAPO) AL CODA Go back to the beginning; then skip to the coda

D.C. (DA CAPO) AL FINE Go back to the beginning and play until Fine

DIMINUENDO (⊃) Get softer gradually

D.S. (DAL SEGNO) AL CODA Go back to the sign 𝄋; then skip to the coda

D.S. (DAL SEGNO) AL FINE Go back to the sign 𝄋 and play until Fine

DUKAS, PAUL French composer (1865–1935)

DVOŘÁK, ANTONIN Czech composer (1841–1904)

ENHARMONICS Any two notes that are written differently, but sound the same. (F♯ = G♭)

FERMATA (𝄐) Hold the note longer

FLAT (♭) Lowers the pitch of a note one half step

FORTE (*f*) Loud

f – p Play loud the first time and soft the second time

FORTISSIMO (*ff*) Very loud

FOSTER, STEPHEN American composer (1826–1864)

GOUNOD, CHARLES French composer (1818–1893)

GRACE NOTE A quick note, usually played just before the beat

GRIEG, EDVARD Norwegian composer (1843–1907)

HALF STEP The distance between any two adjacent keys on the piano

HANDEL, GEORGE F. English composer of German birth (1685–1759)

HERBERT, VICTOR American composer (1859–1924)

JOPLIN, SCOTT American composer (1868–1917)

KEY SIGNATURE Indicates notes which are to be flatted or sharped throughout

LARGO Very slow

MAESTOSO In a majestic style

MEZZO FORTE (*mf*) Medium loud

MEZZO PIANO (*mp*) Medium soft

MENDELSSOHN, FELIX German composer (1809–1847)

MODERATO Medium tempo

MOLTO RIT. Dramatically slow down the tempo

MORLEY, THOMAS English composer (1559–1602)

MOZART, WOLFGANG A. Austrian composer (1756–1791)

MUSSORGSKY, MODEST Russian composer (1839–1881)

NATURAL (♮) Cancels a flat or sharp until the next bar line

OFFENBACH, JACQUES French composer (1819–1880)

PIANISSIMO (*pp*) Very soft

PIANO (*p*) Soft

RACHMANINOFF, SERGEI Russian composer (1873–1943)

RIMSKY-KORSAKOV, NICOLAI Russian composer (1844–1908)

RITARDANDO (RIT.) Gradually slow down the tempo

ROSSINI, GIOACCHINO Italian composer (1792–1868)

SHARP (♯) Raises the pitch of a note one half step

SCHUBERT, FRANZ German composer (1797–1828)

SFORZANDO (*sfz*) A strong accent

SOUSA, JOHN PHILIP American composer (1854–1932)

STACCATO (·) Play the note ½ its normal length

TCHAIKOVSKY, PETER I. Russian composer (1840–1893)

TENUTO (–) Hold the note for its full value

TRANSPOSING Rewriting a melody, beginning on a different starting pitch.

VERDI, GIUSEPPE Italian composer (1813–1901)

VIVACE Very fast tempo

VIVALDI, ANTONIO Italian composer (1678–1741)

WAGNER, RICHARD German composer (1813–1883)

WHOLE STEP Two half steps

BASSOON FINGERING CHART

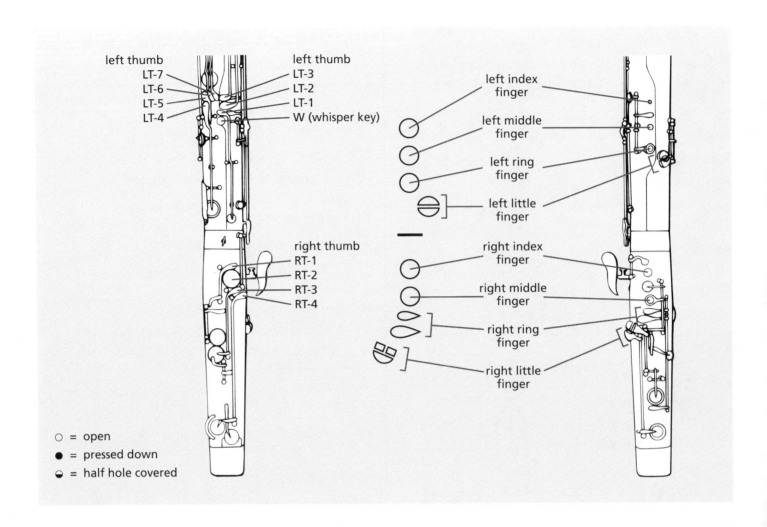

left thumb
LT-7
LT-6
LT-5
LT-4

left thumb
LT-3
LT-2
LT-1
W (whisper key)

right thumb
RT-1
RT-2
RT-3
RT-4

left index finger
left middle finger
left ring finger
left little finger

right index finger
right middle finger
right ring finger
right little finger

○ = open
● = pressed down
◒ = half hole covered

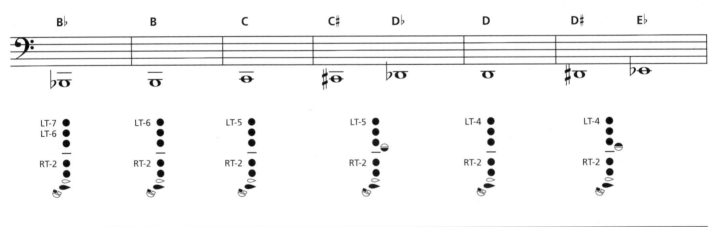

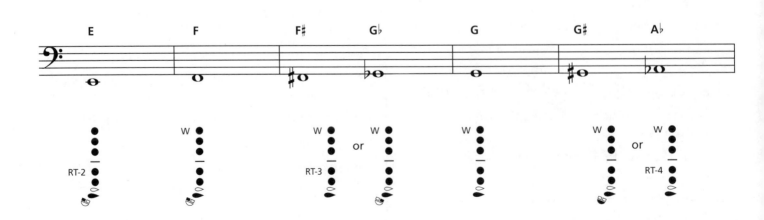

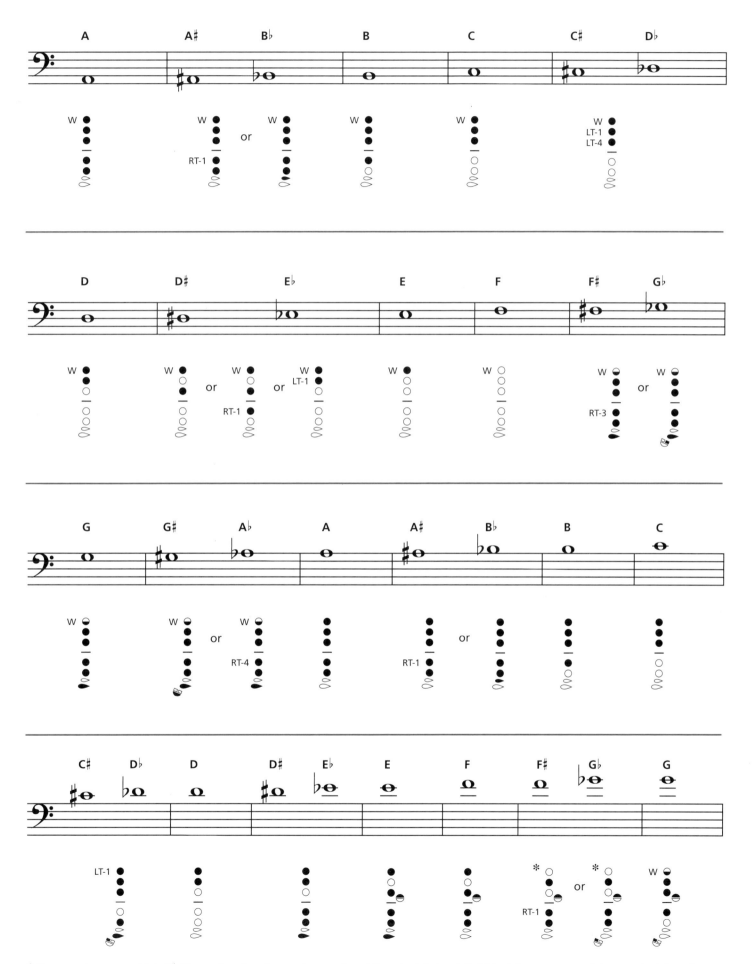

*On some bassoons, high F♯/G♭ can be played more in tune by adding the left hand 3rd (ring) finger to one of the standard fingerings.

HOME PRACTICE RECORD

Week	Date	ASSIGNMENT	Mon	Tue	Wed	Thur	Fri	Sat	Sun	Total	Parent Signature
1											
2											
3											
4											
5											
6											
7											
8											
9											
10											
11											
12											
13											
14											
15											
16											
17											
18											
19											
20											
21											
22											
23											
24											
25											
26											
27											
28											
29											
30											
31											
32											
33											
34											
35											
36	Date	ASSIGNMENT	Mon	Tue	Wed	Thur	Fri	Sat	Sun	Total	